plates to share

SIMPLY DELICIOUS MEALS TO ENJOY WITH FRIENDS plates to share

Jennifer Joyce   photography by Peter Cassidy

RYLAND
PETERS
& SMALL

LONDON NEW YORK

Dedication
To my great friend Victoria Blashford-Snell—my food soul mate.

Design, photographic art direction, and prop styling Steve Painter
Commissioning Editor Julia Charles
Production Controller Paul Harding
Publishing Director Alison Starling

Food Stylist Sunil Vijayakar
Index Hilary Bird

Author's acknowledgements
Once again I'm indebted to my husband Patrick and two sons Liam and Riley for their superior taste-testing skills and helpful feedback. Thanks to my long-time friend and fellow cook, Maarit Visbal, for inspiring me about Scandinavian eating. Thank you to Julia Charles for all her work and help on threading the ideas together for this book, to Sunil Vijayakar for making such lovely food, to Peter Cassidy for the beautiful photographs, Steve Painter for the stunning design, and to Alison Starling for giving me another fabulous book to write.

Printed in China

First published in the United Kingdom in 2008 by Ryland Peters & Small
519 Broadway, 5th Floor,
New York, NY 10012
www.rylandpeters.com

10 9 8 7 6 5 4 3 2

Text © Jennifer Joyce 2008
Design and photographs © Ryland Peters & Small 2008

Library of Congress Cataloging-in-Publication Data

Joyce, Jennifer.
  Plates to share : simply delicious meals to share with friends / Jennifer Joyce ; with photography by Peter Cassidy. -- 1st ed.
      p. cm.
  Includes index.
  ISBN 978-1-84597-630-9
  1. Appetizers. 2. Cookery, International. 3. Entertaining. I. Title.
  TX740.J684 2008
  641.8'12--dc22

2007042987

Notes
• All spoon measurements are level unless otherwise specified.
• Ovens should be preheated to the specified temperatures. All ovens work slightly differently. I recommend using an oven thermometer and suggest you consult the maker's handbook for any special instructions—particularly if you are using a fan-assisted oven as you may need to adjust cooking temperatures according to maker's instructions.
• To sterilize bottles and jars, wash well in soapy water, rinse thoroughly, then boil in plenty of water for 10 minutes. They should be filled as soon as they are dry, and still hot. (If the preserve is cold, let the bottle or jar cool before filling.) For more information on preserving and food safety, go to: http://hgic.clemson.edu/food.htm

contents

introduction

Having friends around to eat no longer means that you must produce a three-course meal. Times are changing and informal food has now moved from the dining room to the coffee table. Buying and arranging small bites is the new, no-fuss way to entertain. *Plates to Share* is all about lacing together bits and pieces from a deli or the pantry, plating them stylishly, and letting people talk, drink, and graze all evening. A deft hand in the kitchen is not required, only smart shopping and a little artistic arrangement. Although I'm passionate about cooking, this is one of my favorite ways to entertain mid-week. It's relaxing for both my guests and me and people are always wowed by what I can put together at short notice.

These small dishes go by many names—meze, hors d'oeuvres, antipasti, and tapas—but they all share a similar history, which began with people socializing and having a small bite to eat before a larger meal. This culinary ritual has now grown so popular it has almost eclipsed the meal itself! *Plates to Share* offers 12 great menus. They are intended to be guidelines and offer inspiration, so don't fret if you can't get hold of a particular item. Bring home your favorites and perhaps make one or two of the recipes to make things a little more special and individual. Although you should be able to buy most things at the supermarket, you may need to look in a deli, ethnic specialty shop, or online gourmet store for the more unusual foods. Top-quality ingredients are the key to pulling this way of entertaining together so buy the very best you can afford and remember that it pays to read the labels—for example, choose olives or marinated vegetables that are packaged in extra-virgin olive oil, not vegetable. Happy shopping and sharing!

classic Italian antipasti

The Italian phrase, "l'arte d'arrangiarsi" (the art of making something out of nothing)
best describes antipasti. It's all about bringing together simple foods to create
a visual treat and a feast of flavors and textures. Simple grilled and pickled
vegetables, spicy salami, and salty cheeses are all good foods when eaten on
their own, but when brought together as antipasti they become a culinary
masterpiece. Find your nearest Italian grocer and take full advantage of the
delicious fresh deli foods and imported goods. Arrange your bounty on wooden
chopping boards and in little dishes, and serve with generous glasses of Chianti.

TO BUY

- Italian-style marinated green olives
- *Cippoline agrodulce* (little onions pickled in sweet balsamic vinegar)
- Large caperberries with stems
- Fresh red and/or green pesto
- Pepperoni sausage
- Napoli and Milano salami
- Marinated grilled artichoke hearts
- Roasted red and yellow bell peppers
- Grilled zucchini slices
- Parmesan and/or pecorino cheese
- Balsamic vinegar and extra-virgin olive oil, to drizzle
- Fresh basil leaves, to garnish
- A selection of rustic Italian breads including *grissini* (breadsticks)

TO PREPARE

- Fresh figs wrapped with *bresaola* (Italian air-dried beef)
- Slices of honeydew melon wrapped with thin slices of *prosciutto* (Italian smoked ham)
- Salad of baby arugula with Parmesan shavings

TO COOK (see recipes pages 10–11)

- Classic tomato and basil bruschetta
- Little sausage-stuffed mushrooms
- Sicilian pepper oil

classic tomato and basil bruschetta

15 thick slices of ciabatta or sourdough bread

1 garlic clove, peeled

4 large, ripe plum tomatoes, seeded and diced

a small handful of basil leaves, torn

freshly squeezed juice of ½ lemon

5 tablespoons extra-virgin olive oil

1 shallot, finely chopped

Parmesan shavings, to garnish

sea salt and freshly ground black pepper

MAKES 15

Preheat the oven to 400°F. Place the slices of bread on a lightly oiled baking sheet and toast them in the preheated oven for 7–8 minutes, until just golden. Rub each one with the clove of garlic and then finely chop what remains. Brush each bruschetta with olive oil and set aside. In a small bowl, mix together the tomatoes, basil, lemon juice, chopped garlic, and shallot. Season well with salt and pepper and mix together. Spoon the tomato mixture on to the bruschetta and top with Parmesan shavings. Serve immediately, while still crispy.

little sausage-stuffed mushrooms

20 white mushrooms, washed and stems removed

5 oz. fresh Italian sausage, casings removed

6 tablespoons homemade breadcrumbs

1 tablespoon freshly grated lemon zest

½ teaspoon crushed fennel seeds

½ teaspoon dried red pepper flakes

2 tablespoons grated Parmesan cheese

2 tablespoons finely chopped flatleaf parsley (plus extra to garnish)

sea salt and freshly ground black pepper

MAKES 20

Preheat the oven to 400°F. In a bowl, mix together the sausagemeat, breadcrumbs, lemon zest, fennel seeds, red pepper flakes, Parmesan, and parsley and season well with salt and pepper.

Stuff each mushroom liberally with the mixture. Season again and place on a lightly oiled baking sheet. Bake in the preheated oven for 15–20 minutes until golden. Sprinkle each mushroom with a little chopped parsley and serve while still hot.

Sicilian pepper oil

250 ml extra-virgin olive oil

2 garlic cloves, finely chopped

1 tablespoon dried red pepper flakes

4 sun-dried tomatoes, finely chopped

1 tablespoon fennel seeds

1 tablespoon Sicilian or Greek dried oregano

1 teaspoon each sea salt and freshly ground black pepper

Heat the oil in a skillet over low heat and add the garlic and red pepper flakes. When the garlic turns golden, add all the remaining ingredients and remove from the heat. Cover the pan and let the mixture cool at room temperature. When cool, pour into a sterilized bottle or jar and refrigerate until ready to use it. The oil will keep in the fridge for up to two weeks.

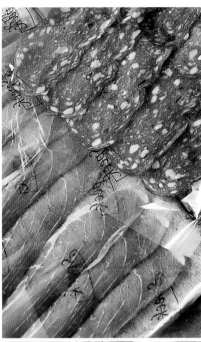

Spanish tapas

Tapas were originally an accompaniment for an early evening drink, the name deriving from the word "tapa" (lid)—a small dish containing a few small bites that was placed on top of a glass. Bite-size pieces of salty cheese with chunks of sweet quince preserve, slices of spicy chorizo, and sour caperberries—these snacks will make your taste buds sing. You can buy most things in a supermarket but for inspiration do visit a Spanish specialty market. Look out for the *jamón Ibérico* (cured ham from acorn-fed pigs), spicy-sweet *piquillo* peppers, and heart-shaped Marcona almonds. Serve up your finds in traditional terracotta dishes (*cazuelas*), or colorful plates. A dainty glass of chilled Manzanilla or raisin-scented Oloroso sherry could be served or, if you prefer wine, try Vega-Sicilia's "Unico" Ribera del Duero or any Rioja.

TO BUY

- Hams, such as *serrano* and *Ibérico*
- Chorizo sausage
- Marinated fresh anchovies with garlic
- Large caperberries with stalks
- Manchego cheese and a block of *membrillo* (quince preserve)
- Roasted and salted Marcona almonds
- Oven-roasted *piquillo* peppers in oil
- Pimento-stuffed large green olives
- Prepared gazpacho soup (to serve in shot glasses, see picture on page 14)
- A loaf of good white bread, thickly sliced, or crusty white rolls

TO PREPARE

- Endive leaves filled with mashed *Cabrales* (Spanish soft blue cheese) and sprinkled with chopped walnuts
- Black olives tossed with olive oil, freshly grated orange zest, crushed whole garlic, and dried red pepper flakes
- Baby new potatoes, boiled in slightly salted water and tossed with Saffron and Garlic Aïoli (see page 21)
- Fresh mussels, cleaned and steamed in fish broth with a dash of Spanish sherry and a minced garlic clove

TO COOK (see recipes pages 14–17)

- Fresh asparagus with aioli
- Pan-fried green peppers
- Roasted red pepper, tuna, and egg salad
- Potatoes in spicy sauce
- Spanish omelette
- Sherried chicken livers
- Shrimp with garlic

fresh asparagus with aioli
esparragos con aioli

2 bunches thin asparagus, trimmed

2 egg yolks, at room temperature

1 teaspoon Dijon mustard

½ teaspoon each salt and pepper

2 teaspoons *pimentón dulce* (Spanish sweet smoked paprika)

1 garlic clove, crushed

¾ cup grapeseed or sunflower oil

1 tablespoon freshly squeezed lemon juice

MAKES 1¼ CUPS AIOLI

Blanch the asparagus in salted water for 2 minutes. Drain and immediately place in a bowl of cold water to refresh. Drain again and dry on paper towels. Put the egg yolks, salt, pepper, pimentón, and garlic in a bowl and whisk to combine. While still whisking, slowly drizzle in the oil until incorporated. Add the lemon juice and whisk again. Serve a bowl of aioli as a dip with the asparagus.

pan-fried green peppers
pimientos de Padrón

5 oz. Padrón peppers or other small green peppers, such as poblanos

2 tablespoons extra-virgin olive oil

1–2 teaspoons sea salt flakes

SERVES 4–6

Heat the olive oil in a large, heavy-based skillet until very hot. Add the peppers and cook them over high heat for 2–3 minutes, shaking the pan to stop them catching and burning. As soon as they puff up and start to brown, remove from the heat and sprinkle generously with the sea salt flakes. Serve while warm.

roasted red pepper, tuna, and egg salad
ensalada de pimiento asado, atun, y huevos

5–6 *piquillo* roasted red peppers, cut into pieces

3 oz. tuna fillet, packed in olive oil

2 eggs, hard-boiled and quartered

1 small red onion, finely sliced

8 black olives, stoned

1 tablespoon sherry vinegar

3 tablespoons extra-virgin olive oil

2 tablespoons chopped flatleaf parsley

sea salt and freshly ground black pepper

SERVES 4–6

Place the peppers on a serving plate. Arrange the tuna, eggs, onion, and olives on top. Drizzle with the vinegar and oil and season to taste with salt and pepper. Let the salad sit for 10 minutes and sprinkle with the parsley just before serving.

potatoes in spicy sauce
patatas bravas

10 small red potatoes, peeled

7 tablespoons olive oil

1 small onion, finely chopped

2 garlic cloves, finely chopped

2 teaspoons *pimentón dulce* (Spanish sweet smoked paprika)

1 teaspoon ground cumin

1 tablespoon mild chili powder

14-oz. can Italian plum tomatoes, puréed

1 tablespoon sherry vinegar

sea salt and freshly ground black pepper

SERVES 4–6

Preheat the oven to 400°F. Boil the potatoes in salted water until just tender. Drain and when cool enough to handle, cut into quarters. Place on a baking sheet and drizzle with 3 tablespoons of the olive oil. Season well with salt and pepper and bake in the preheated oven for about 40 minutes, until crisp.

Gently heat the remaining olive oil in a large saucepan. Add the onion and garlic and sauté for a few minutes. Add all of the remaining ingredients, season to taste with salt and pepper and stir as the sauce warms through. Pour the sauce over the potatoes and sprinkle with parsley to serve.

Spanish omelette
tortilla español

2 cups extra-virgin olive oil

2 large yellow onions, thinly sliced

1½ large waxy potatoes

6 eggs

2 tablespoons chicken or vegetable broth

sea salt and freshly ground black pepper

SERVES 6–8

Heat 3 tablespoons of the olive oil in a large, heavy-based skillet. Add the onions and season well. Cook for a few minutes over high heat then reduce the heat to low and cook for a further 30 minutes, stirring often to prevent them from burning. Remove the onions from the pan and set aside. Cut the potatoes into chunks about 1 inch thick. Sprinkle with sea salt. Heat the remaining oil in a large skillet and add the potato chunks. Cook them over low heat for about 25 minutes, turning occasionally, until soft. Use a slotted spoon to remove them from the pan and set aside. Discard all but 3 tablespoons of the cooking oil and return the pan to high heat. Whisk the eggs and stock in a large bowl and add a pinch of salt. Tip the onions and potatoes into the egg mixture and stir gently to combine. Transfer the mixture to the pan and use the back of a spoon to flatten the surface. Reduce the heat to medium/low and cook for about 8 minutes, until the tortilla is fairly solid. Top the pan with a large plate and invert the tortilla. Gently slide it back into the pan to cook for 3–4 more minutes on the other side, until the center is cooked. Slide the tortilla on to a plate and once cool, cut into slices or small squares to serve.

sherried chicken livers
higados al jerez

14 oz. chicken livers, trimmed

1 tablespoon olive oil

1 garlic clove, finely chopped

3 tablespoons sweet sherry

freshly squeezed juice and finely grated zest of 1 lemon

a handful of flatleaf parsley, chopped

sea salt and freshly ground black pepper

SERVES 4–6

Slice the livers into bite-size pieces and season with salt and pepper. Heat the olive oil in a large skillet. Add the garlic and sauté for 1 minute. Add the livers and brown them on both sides. Pour in the sherry and lemon juice. Gently cook until there is no more liquid and then stir in the lemon zest and parsley. Serve warm, on toothpicks.

shrimp with garlic
gambas al ajillo

¼ cup olive oil

3 garlic cloves, finely chopped

½ teaspoon dried red pepper flakes

14 oz. large raw shrimp, peeled

1 tablespoon dry sherry

2 tablespoons chopped flatleaf parsley

SERVES 4–6

Heat the oil in a skillet. Add the
garlic and red pepper flakes and
sauté until just golden. Add the
shrimp and cook for 1–2 minutes
over high heat. Pour in the sherry
and cook for another 1–2 minutes,
until the shrimp are opaque and
cooked through. Remove from
the heat, sprinkle with parsley
and serve.

Provençal crudités platter
"le grand aïoli"

This extravaganza originates from Provence in the South of the France and is a glorious celebration of the region's produce. Traditionally, a selection of raw or blanched baby vegetables and hard-cooked eggs are served with a rich, garlicky sauce for dipping—the aïoli which gives this feast its name. Arrange the vegetables on a large oval platter and serve the dip in a bowl, then let your guests help themselves. I've included some recipes for alternative dips here too, so that you can ring the changes. Enjoy with a glass of chilled unwooded Chardonnay or a dry rosé.

TO PREPARE

- Baby carrots with tops left on
- Radishes with stems and leaves left on
- Cucumber, sliced into thick batons
- Scallions, trimmed
- Fennel, quartered and sliced
- Celery hearts with leaves left on
- Sugar snap peas or snow peas

- Green or string beans, blanched
- Cherry tomatoes on the vine
- Red or yellow bell peppers, cut into strips
- Organic eggs, hard-cooked and halved
- A large loaf of good French country bread, ideally the Provençal *fougasse* also known as "ladder" bread

TO MAKE (see recipes on page 21)

- Saffron and garlic aïoli
- Goat cheese, onion, and herb dip
- Beetroot, horseradish, and crème fraîche dip
- Warm anchovy and lemon dip

Or you could also try:

- Lime and caper mayonnaise (see page 51)
- Sicilian pepper oil (see page 11)

saffron and garlic aïoli

2 egg yolks, at room temperature

1 teaspoon Dijon mustard

1 teaspoon crushed saffron threads, soaked in 1 tablespoon lukewarm water

1 garlic clove, crushed

½ teaspoon each sea salt and freshly ground black pepper

¾ cup grapeseed or sunflower oil

1 tablespoon freshly squeezed lemon juice

MAKES 1¼ CUPS

Put the egg yolks in a bowl or food processor and add the mustard, saffron, garlic, and salt and pepper. While whisking, or with the motor running, slowly drizzle in the oil until it is all incorporated. Add the lemon juice and mix again. This keeps for four days, refrigerated.

goat cheese, onion, and herb dip

6½ oz. soft, mild chevre (goat cheese)

¼ cup light cream

2 scallions, finely chopped

1 teaspoon freshly grated lemon zest

1 tablespoon each of finely chopped chives, fresh thyme, and fresh tarragon

sea salt and freshly ground black pepper

MAKES 1¼ CUPS

Put all the ingredients in a bowl and, using a fork, mix well to combine. Season to taste with salt and pepper and transfer to a serving bowl. Chill slightly before serving. This keeps for three days, refrigerated

beet, horseradish, and crème fraîche dip

6 oz. cooked beets

2 tablespoons hot horseradish (freshly grated if possible)

¾ cup crème fraîche or sour cream

sea salt and freshly ground black pepper

MAKES 2 CUPS

Put all of the ingredients in a blender and pulse until smooth. Season to taste with salt and pepper and transfer to a serving bowl. Chill before serving. This keeps for three days, refrigerated.

warm anchovy and lemon dip

2 tablespoons unsalted butter

½ cup extra-virgin olive oil

3 garlic cloves, finely chopped

4 large anchovies, packed in olive oil, drained and chopped

rind of ½ unwaxed lemon, finely chopped

3 teaspoons freshly squeezed lemon juice

½ teaspoon crushed dried red pepper flakes

2 tablespoons finely chopped flatleaf parsley

freshly ground black pepper

MAKES ¾ CUP

Heat the oil and butter in a small saucepan. Add the garlic, anchovies, and lemon and simmer over low heat for 4–5 minutes, until the garlic is golden. Add the lemon juice, red pepper flakes, and parsley and season to taste with black pepper. Keep warm over very low heat until ready to serve. This keeps for four days, refrigerated.

Italian crostini plate

Italian in origin, "crostini" translates literally as "little crusts." These rounds of bread are brushed with olive oil, and sometimes garlic, then baked in the oven to make them delectably crispy. They make dainty and colorful, bite-size appetizers that are perfect to share with friends. Crostini bases make an ideal vehicle for most Italian deli foods—top them with velvety cheeses, smoky grilled vegetables, fresh seafood, and glossy olives, then jazz things up with fresh lemon zest and fresh basil. You can try my suggested flavor combinations or try creating your own. The bread is pivotal though. Good-quality baguettes, sourdough bread, and rustic ciabatta are ideal, but stay clear of the lesser-quality breads as they will produce a rock hard texture. Enjoy with a glass of Italian red, such as Valpolicella, Amarone, or Brunello.

IDEAS

- Cheeses, such as ricotta, Gorgonzola, goat cheese, provolone, and mozzarella

- Italian cured meats such as *bresaola*, *prosciutto*, and salami

- Fish and seafood such as anchovy fillets, cooked shrimp, and crabmeat

- Salad greens and vegetables such as arugula, radicchio, endive, and fennel

- Marinated Italian antipasti vegetables, such as artichoke hearts, mushrooms, eggplant, and roasted bell peppers

- Italian-style herb-marinated olives

- Pickled vegetables sush as baby gherkins, *peperoncini* (pickled chile peppers), and *cippoline agrodulce* (little onions pickled in sweet balsamic vinegar)

- Fresh fruit such as figs, peaches, pears, and grapes—all delicious with cheese

- Fresh herbs for sprinkling—such as basil and flatleaf parsley

- Extra-virgin olive oil and aged balsamic vinegar for drizzling

TO MAKE (see recipes pages 24–25)

- Gorgonzola, cherry tomato, and basil

- Spicy shrimp with lemon and radicchio

- Ricotta, fig, and *bresaola*

- Goat cheese, *prosciutto*, and artichoke

- Roasted red bell pepper, borlotti bean, and arugula

- Crab, lemon, chiles, avocado, and arugula

- Salami, fennel, provolone, and *peperoncini*

- Asparagus, mozzarella, yellow bell pepper, and black olive

the crostini base

Preheat the oven to 400°F. Slice a baguette into slices about 1 inch thick. Place them on a non-stick baking sheet and brush with olive oil. Bake for 6 minutes, until browned on the edges but still chewy in the center.

EACH RECIPE TOPS 4–6 SMALL TOASTS

ricotta, fig, and *bresaola*

Spread the toasts with a little fresh ricotta. Top each with a folded piece of *bresaola* and a slice of ripe fig. Season with salt and pepper and sprinkle a little chopped basil on top to serve.

crab, lemon, chile, avocado, and arugula

Mix a large handful of crabmeat with 1 tablespoon of chopped hot red chile and 1 tablespoon olive oil. Place a couple of avocado slices on the toast, and top with a spoonful of crab mixture and some arugula. Squeeze lemon juice over the top.

Gorgonzola, cherry tomato, and basil

Spread the toasts with Gorgonzola cheese and top each with a few halves of cherry tomatoes. Drizzle with extra-virgin olive oil. Season with salt and pepper and sprinkle a little chopped basil on top to serve.

goat cheese, *prosciutto*, and artichoke

Spread the toasts with any soft, mild goat cheese such as chevre. Top each one with some *prosciutto* and a piece of marinated artichoke heart. Season with cracked black pepper to serve.

salami, fennel, provolone, and *peperoncini*

Top each toast with a slice of provolone cheese, 2–3 pieces of spicy Italian salami, such as *Napoli piccante*, and a few thin slices of raw fennel. Sprinkle with a little chopped *peperoncini* to serve.

spicy shrimp with lemon and radicchio

Mix two large handfuls of small cooked shrimp with 1 tablespoon extra-virgin olive oil, the juice and zest of ½ lemon, 2 tablespoons chopped parsley, and 1 tablespoon chopped hot red chile. Place a small handful of chopped radicchio on each toast and top with a spoonful of the shrimp mixture. Season with salt and pepper to serve.

roasted red bell pepper, borlotti bean, and arugula

Sauté 1 sliced garlic clove and 1 anchovy fillet in 2 tablespoons olive oil until golden. Add a large handful each of chopped roasted red bell peppers and canned borlotti beans. Season the mixture with salt and pepper to taste and spoon on to the toasts. Top with Parmesan shavings and a few arugula leaves to serve.

asparagus, mozzarella, yellow bell pepper, and black olive

Drain 2 fresh buffalo mozzarella balls and them rip into pieces. Top each toast with some mozzarella, 2–3 tips of grilled baby asparagus, a few slices of roasted yellow bell pepper and 1–2 pitted black olives. Season with salt and pepper to taste. Drizzle with a little extra-virgin olive to serve.

Middle Eastern mezze

Taking its inspiration from the little meze dishes of Lebanon, Syria, and Egypt, this is the perfect party menu. Exotic fragrant spices, fresh green herbs, and citrus are the key flavors and will make your house smell like heaven. It is the ultimate finger food as lots of scooping, dipping, and eating with your hands is involved— you'll need plenty of flatbread. Do try and buy some *dukkah*. This is a delicious blend of spices nuts and seeds that is eaten by dipping fresh bread or quail's eggs first into olive oil and then into the mixture. For dessert, put together a beautiful platter of sticky-sweet dates, fresh figs, pomegranates, and giant sultanas. Serve with mint tea in ornate glasses or some cherry-scented Lebanese Syrah red wine.

TO BUY IN

- Prepared *tabbouleh* or other bulgur wheat salad with fresh parsley and mint

- *Dukkah* (a Middle Eastern dip that is a dry mixture of chopped nuts, seeds, cumin, and coriander)

- Quail's eggs (to dip in the *dukkah*)

- *Labneh* (a Lebanese soft cheese made from yoghurt) drizzled with olive oil and sprinkled with fresh parsley

- Pita, *khubz*, or any other Middle Eastern flatbread

- Pistachios and giant golden raisins

- Dates, fresh figs, and pomegranates

TO PREPARE

- A simple salad of fresh orange slices, black olives, and thinly sliced red onion

- Olives and red bell pepper slices tossed in oil and garnished with toasted cumin seeds and wedges of fresh lemon

- Flavored flatbreads: sprinkle a flatbread with *za'atar* (a Middle Eastern spice blend), or a mixture of dried thyme and toasted white sesame seeds. Drizzle with olive oil, heat under the broiler for 2 minutes and cut into wedges

TO COOK (see recipes pages 28–31)

- Spicy chicken skewers

- Crumbled cheese dip with herbs and pomegranate seeds

- Lebanese hot red pepper and walnut dip (*muhummara*)

- Eggplant slices in spiced honey sauce

- Mini lamb meatballs (*kibbe*)

spicy chicken skewers

3 boneless and skinless chicken thighs

1 tablespoon *harissa* paste (fiery-hot chile paste)

1 teaspoon cumin seeds

1 tablespoon finely grated fresh ginger

1 tablespoon honey

½ cup olive oil

sea salt and freshly ground black pepper

TO SERVE:

labneh (see page 27)

lemon wedges, to squeeze

romaine lettuce leaves

flatbread

25 metal skewers or wooden skewers, soaked in water for 20 minutes

MAKES 25

Cut the chicken into bite-size pieces. Mix all the other ingredients together in a medium bowl and add the chicken. Toss until the chicken pieces are coated. Season well with salt and pepper. Set aside to marinate for at least 1 hour.

When ready to cook, thread the chicken on to the skewers, adding about three pieces to each. Heat a stove-top grill pan or outdoor grill. Cook the chicken for 2–3 minutes on each side until browned. Serve with plain yoghurt and sliced red onion.

crumbled cheese dip
with herbs and
pomegranate seeds

10 oz. feta cheese, crumbled

freshly squeezed juice of 1 lemon

5 tablespoons extra-virgin olive oil

a pinch of dried red pepper flakes

1 small red onion, finely diced

1 tablespoon each finely chopped parsley, dill, and mint

2 tablespoons pomegranate molasses

4 tablespoons pomegranate seeds

MAKES 1½ CUPS

Arrange the crumbled cheese in a serving bowl. Pour the lemon juice and olive oil over it. Sprinkle the red pepper flakes, onion, and herbs on top. Drizzle with the pomegranate molasses and sprinkle with the seeds to finish. Serve with warmed flatbread for dipping.

Lebanese hot red pepper and walnut dip
muhammara

1 cup shelled walnuts, toasted

6½ oz. *piquillo* roasted red peppers

1 garlic clove, crushed

1 teaspoon *pimentón picante* (hot smoked Spanish paprika)

1 teaspoon ground cumin

1 tablespoon tomato paste

1 tablespoon red wine vinegar

2 tablespoons pomegranate molasses

6 tablespoons extra-virgin olive oil

fresh pomegranate seeds, to serve

sea salt and freshly ground black pepper

SERVES 4–6

Put the walnuts, peppers, and garlic in a food processor or blender. Process to a paste and then add the pimentón, cumin, tomato paste, vinegar, and pomegranate molasses. Season well with salt and pepper and blend again. With the motor running, slowly pour in the olive oil until it is incorporated. If the mixture is too thick, add a few tablespoons of water or lemon juice. Serve sprinkled with fresh pomegranate seeds.

eggplant slices in spiced honey sauce

2 medium eggplants

¼ cup olive oil

3 garlic cloves

2-inch piece of fresh ginger, finely grated

1½ teaspoons ground cumin

½ teaspoon cayenne pepper or hot chili powder

6 tablespoons honey

freshly squeezed juice of 1 lemon

⅔ cup water

chopped flatleaf parsley, to serve

sea salt

SERVES 4

Preheat the broiler to high. Peel the eggplants and cut them into rounds about ½ inch thick. Dip them in olive oil, turning them over, and sprinkle with salt. Cook under the hot broiler, turning them over once, until they are lightly browned. Put the garlic and ginger in a large skillet with the remaining oil and sauté for 1–2 minutes, until golden. Add the cumin, cayenne pepper, honey, lemon juice, and water and cook for another 2 minutes. Add the egplant slices and cook over low heat for about 10 minutes, until they are soft. Sprinkle with the chopped parsley to serve.

mini lamb meatballs
kibbe

⅔ cup bulgur or cracked wheat

1 lb. ground lamb

1 small onion, finely chopped

½ teaspoon each ground cumin, allspice, and cinnamon

olive oil, to drizzle

sea salt and freshly ground black pepper

TO SERVE:

Greek yoghurt with chopped fresh dill

MAKES 25

Preheat the broiler to high. Soak the bulgur for 20 minutes in enough cold water to cover it. Put the lamb, onion, and spices in a bowl and season with salt and pepper. Drain the bulgur and squeeze out as much water as you can. Add the bulgur to the lamb and mix well. Use your hands to shape the mixture into small balls or sausage shapes. Place the kibbe on a nonstick baking sheet and drizzle with olive oil. Roll them around so that they are well coated and season with salt and pepper. Place the sheet under the preheated broiler and brown on one side (about 6–7 minutes) and then turn over and grill for another 5 minutes. Serve warm, with the yoghurt and dill on the side.

Arabesque feast

A feast for the eyes and well as the senses, this menu takes its inspiration from the food of the Eastern Mediterranean and North Africa and features the best of Turkish and Lebanese *meze,* as well as the Moroccan equivalent, *kemia.* The dishes are similar in style to Middle Eastern mezze, as these cuisines make the most of fragrant spices, fresh green herbs, and zesty citrus fruit, but they also feature flaky phyllo pastry and scented rosewater. This is lovely served with raki, a Turkish aniseed-flavored aperitif, but you could drink a crisp white wine if you prefer. Why not buy some crumbly sesame seed *halva* or sticky Turkish *baklava* (sweet pastries) to serve at the end of your meal with little cups of strong coffee.

TO BUY

- Prepared hummus, drizzled with olive oil and sprinkled with toasted sesame seeds

- Prepared *baba ghanoush* (a smoky eggplant dip) sprinkled with pimentón dulce (mild smoked Spanish paprika) and chopped parsley

- Falafel (chickpea fritters)

- Toasted pita and/or *lavash* (crispy flatbread)

- Fresh dates and a selection of halva (sesame sweets) and baklava (sweet pastries)

TO PREPARE

- A simple salad of cooked beets, diced orange flesh, and chopped fresh cilantro, dressed with oil and vinegar

- Cooked fava beans tossed with fresh dill, crumbled feta, and freshly squeezed lemon juice

- Toasted pomegranate seeds, sprinkled with rosewater

TO COOK (see recipes pages 34–37)

- Spicy chicken wings with lemon and garlic

- Grilled eggplant slices with green beans and pomegranate molasses

- Lebanese bread salad (*fattoush*)

- Turkish bulgur salad (*kisir*)

- Spinach, cinnamon, and pine nut phyllo cigars (*börek*)

- Warm halloumi bites

spicy chicken wings with lemon and garlic

12–15 chicken wings

5 garlic cloves, crushed

3 tablespoons extra-virgin olive oil

freshly squeezed juice and zest of
1 unwaxed lemon

½ teaspoon ground allspice

½ teaspoon cayenne pepper

lemon wedges, to serve

SERVES 4–6

Using poultry scissors or a knife, cut the chicken wings at the knuckle into two pieces. Alternatively, you can ask your butcher to do this.

Mix all the remaining ingredients together in a large bowl. Add the chicken pieces and toss until coated in the mixture. Marinate, refrigerated, for a minimum of 1 hour and up to 12 hours. When ready to cook, preheat the broiler to high. Broil the wings for about 5 minutes on each side, until crisp on the edges. Serve warm with lemon wedges on the side for squeezing.

grilled eggplant slices with green beans and pomegranate molasses

2 small eggplants

6 tablespoons extra-virgin olive oil

½ teaspoon cinnamon

7 oz. thin green beans, trimmed

1 small red onion, sliced into half moons

2 tablespoons chopped fresh mint

3 tablespoons pomegranate molasses

sea salt and freshly ground black pepper

SERVES 4–6

Cut the eggplants into ½ inch slices. Brush with a little olive oil, sprinkle with the cinnamon, and season with salt and pepper. Heat a ridged grill pan until smoking and cook the eggplant on both sides until black stripes appear. Set aside.

Blanch the green beans in salted water, then drain and refresh them in iced water. Pat them dry with paper towels. Transfer the beans to a large bowl and add the cooked eggplant slices and onion. Toss to mix, then tip on to a serving plate. Drizzle the vegetables with the remaining olive oil and pomegranate molasses. Sprinkle with chopped mint and serve warm or at room temperature.

Lebanese bread salad
fattoush

6 tablespoons olive oil

3 large white or brown pita breads, cut into strips ½-inch wide

2 garlic cloves, finely chopped

freshly squeezed juice of 1 lemon

2 tablespoons each of freshly chopped flat leaf parsley, cilantro, and mint

1 cucumber, peeled, seeded, and diced

1 red onion, finely diced

10 cherry tomatoes, quartered

1 green bell pepper, chopped

½ teaspoon ground sumac

SERVES 4–6

Heat 2 tablespoons of the oil in a skillet and gently fry the pita bread strips until they are golden brown. Drain on paper towels to remove excess oil.

Put the garlic, lemon juice, remaining olive oil, and the herbs in a large bowl and whisk with a fork to combine. Add the cucumber, onion, tomatoes, and green bell pepper. Season well with salt and pepper and toss. Transfer to a serving dish, sprinkle with the sumac, and garnish with strips of crispy bread.

Turkish bulgur salad
kisir

1¼ cups bulgur wheat

5 tablespoons extra-virgin olive oil

6 scallions, thinly sliced

1 tablespoon tomato paste

freshly squeezed juice of 1 lemon

2 tablespoons pomegranate molasses

1 teaspoon cayenne pepper

1 teaspoon dried mint

2 tablespoons chopped flatleaf parsley

1 small cucumber, thinly sliced

2 plum tomatoes, seeded and chopped

sea salt and freshly ground black pepper

Boston lettuce leaves, to serve

SERVES 4–6

Place the bulgur in a large, heatproof bowl and pour ½ cup boiling water over the top. Let it sit for at least 10 minutes, until all the water has been absorbed, and then use a fork to fluff it up.

Add all the other ingredients and season very well with salt and pepper. Mix to combine everything. Serve spooned over a bed of Boston lettuce leaves.

spinach, cinnamon, and pine nut phyllo cigars
börek

4 tablespoons olive oil

1 large onion, finely chopped

3 garlic cloves, finely chopped

½ teaspoon cinnamon

8 oz. fresh spinach, cooked, drained, and roughly chopped

3 tablespoons pine nuts, toasted

8 oz. phyllo pastry, thawed if frozen

melted butter, for brushing pastry

sea salt and freshly ground black pepper

MAKES 20

Heat the olive oil in a skillet over low heat and add the onions. Cook for about 8 minutes, until the onion is soft. Add the garlic and cook gently for a few more minutes. Add the spinach and cinnamon and cook for a further 5 minutes. Transfer the mixture to a bowl and add the pine nuts. Season well with salt and pepper and set aside to cool.

Preheat the oven to 400°F and place a baking sheet in the oven to heat. Take a sheet of phyllo and brush it with melted butter. Place a few teaspoonfuls of the spinach mixture across the lower edge of the pastry, leaving a space of about ¾ inch at each end. Fold the lower edge of the

pastry up, and then bring the sides in. Roll tightly all the way up and then brush with melted butter. Repeat until you have used up all the phyllo and filling. Place the börek on the hot baking sheet and cook in the preheated oven for about 15 minutes, until golden brown. Serve warm.

warm halloumi bites

6½ oz. halloumi cheese, cut into bite-size pieces

2 tablespoons olive oil

2 tablespoons chopped flatleaf parsley

lemon wedges, to serve

wooden toothpicks, to serve (optional)

SERVES 4–6

Heat the olive oil in a skillet until very hot. Working in batches, brown the pieces of halloumi on both sides. Remove them from the pan with a slotted spoon and drain on paper towels to soak up any excess oil. Sprinkle with parsley and serve warm with lemon wedges for squeezing over the top.

Scandinavian fish feast

Scandinavian style is simple, clean and pure—and the same could be said of the region's cuisine. The diet enjoyed in Sweden, Denmark, and Norway has largely been shaped by the climate. Long winters meant that people devoted energy to preserving food by salt-curing, smoking, pickling, and air-drying. A plentiful supply of fish from the sea and freshwater lakes meant that herring, trout, mackerel, and salmon were all treated in some or all of these ways. The resulting flavors are intense and best complemented by fresh or piquant tastes—cucumbers, smoked apples, fresh dill, mustard, and horseradish sauce are all traditional accompaniments. Look out for the crispy Swedish rye flatbread called *tunnbröd* and serve this feast with shot glasses of aquavit (for the brave!) or ice-cold beer.

TO BUY

- A selection of sliced smoked salmon, including marinated *gravadlax* with dill

- Smoked trout slices or fillets and peppered mackerel fillets

- Pickled rollmops or herring fillets

- Creamed horseradish, sweet mustard dill sauce, and apple jelly

- Sprigs of fresh dill and caperberries

- A selection of rye breads including Swedish rye flatbread (*tunnbröd*) and dark rye bread

TO PREPARE

- A simple salad of finely diced tomatoes and sliced red onion

- Chopped hard-cooked egg

- Slices of fresh green apple

- Lemon wedges for squeezing

TO COOK (see recipes pages 40–41)

- Mini roasted potatoes with crème fraîche and caviar

- Warm baby beet salad with mustard seed dressing

- Pickled shrimp

- Cucumber salad with red onion and dill

mini roasted potatoes
with crème fraîche and caviar

24 small new potatoes, halved

3 tablespoons olive oil

¾ cup crème fraîche or sour cream

4 oz. caviar or other fish roe

3 tablespoons finely snipped chives

sea salt and freshly ground black pepper

SERVES 4–6

Preheat the oven to 400°F. Place the potatoes on a large baking sheet and drizzle with olive oil. Season well with salt and pepper. Bake uncovered in the preheated oven for 40 minutes, until crisp.

Serve the potatoes warm, arranged on a plate with small bowls of caviar, crème fraîche, and chives on the side.

warm baby beet salad
with mustard
seed dressing

1 lb. baby beets, uncooked

2 tablespoons red wine vinegar

3 tablespoons extra-virgin olive oil

½ teaspoon yellow mustard seeds

1 shallot, finely chopped

4 scallions, thinly sliced

2 tablespoons finely chopped fresh dill

sea salt and freshly ground black pepper

SERVES 4–6

Put the beets in a large saucepan with plenty of water and boil until easily pierced with a skewer. Drain and set aside. When cool enough to handle, peel the skin off. Cut the beets into quarters and place them in a salad bowl.

To make the dressing, put the vinegar, oil, mustard seeds, and shallot in a small bowl and whisk with a fork to combine. Season to taste with salt and pepper. Pour the dressing over the warm beets and toss gently. Sprinkle with the scallions and dill to serve.

pickled shrimp

14 oz. cooked shrimp

1 red onion, thinly sliced

3 lemons (2 juiced, 1 thinly sliced)

½ cup extra-virgin olive oil

1 tablespoon each of celery seeds, mustard seeds, and fennel seeds

1 teaspoon dried red pepper flakes

6 bay leaves

2 tablespoons white wine vinegar

3 garlic cloves, thinly sliced

SERVES 4–6

Combine all the ingredients in a resealable, non-metal container. Cover and refrigerate for at least 12 hours, turning occasionally. Spoon on to rye bread to serve.

cucumber salad
with red onion and dill

2–3 small cucumbers (Lebanese or other small variety)

1 small red onion, finely diced

2 tablespoons white wine vinegar

3 tablespoons extra-virgin olive oil

½ teaspoon superfine sugar

2 tablespoons finely chopped fresh dill

sea salt and freshly ground black pepper

SERVES 4–6

Cut the cucumbers into thin slices and place them in a salad bowl with the red onion. To make the dressing, put the vinegar, oil and sugar in a separate bowl and season with salt and pepper. Whisk with a fork to combine.

Pour the dressing over the cucumber and onion and sprinkle with the dill to serve.

French *hors d'oeuvres*

French *hors d'oeuvres* are essentially palate "teasers"—a selection of delicious cold foods intended to whet your appetite before a larger meal and often served as a buffet. With some clever shopping and a few simple recipes, you can put together a spread of tasty French treats that makes an indulgent and satisfying meal. Visit your local delicatessen to buy pungent cheeses, cured meats, sausages, pâtés, and terrines and then make some fresh salads and warm dishes at home. It pays to buy the best bread you can get your hands on, so if you are lucky enough to have an artisanal baker nearby, do pay a visit. Lay out your foods artfully on wooden chopping boards and wicker trays to create a rustic feel. You could wash everything down with a chilled white Burgundy or small glasses of aniseed-flavored Pernod.

TO BUY

- Meat pâtés, terrines, and rillettes (potted meat)

- A selection of charcuterie including *saucisson* (sausage) and Bayonne ham

- A selection of cheeses such as Comté, Camembert, Roquefort, and little *chèvre* (goat cheese) balls rolled in herbs

- Pots of prepared pastes—*tapenade* (black olive) and *anchoïade* (anchovy)

- Niçoise-style marinated olives and *cornichons* (pickled baby gherkins)

- French whole grain mustard

- A really good-quality baguette or a sourdough bread, such as *pain au levain*

TO PREPARE

- A simple salad of raw white button mushrooms tossed in classic French vinaigrette and sprinkled with chopped fresh tarragon

- A plate of sliced tomatoes, sprinkled with crumbled blue cheese and walnuts and drizzed with walnut oil and vinegar

- Thin slices of baguette, toasted, spread with *tapenade,* and topped with a few slices of radish

TO COOK (see recipes pages 44–47)

- Baby asparagus with vinaigrette and chopped egg

- Celeriac *rémoulade*

- Blanched green beans with hazelnuts and raspberry vinaigrette

- Cheese, half-dried tomato, and black olive gougères

- Bacon-wrapped prunes stuffed with almonds

- Quick mini *pissaladières* (savory puff pastry tartlets)

baby asparagus
with vinaigrette and chopped egg

2 bunches baby asparagus, trimmed

3 tablespoons extra-virgin olive oil

1 tablespoon red wine vinegar

½ teaspoon Dijon mustard

1 shallot, finely diced

1 egg, hard-cooked

2 tablespoons chopped flatleaf parsley

sea salt and freshly ground black pepper

SERVES 4–6

Blanch the asparagus in a saucepan of salted boiling water. Drain and refresh in cold water. Pat dry with paper towels and arrange in a serving dish.

To make the dressing, put the oil, vinegar, mustard, and shallot in a small bowl and season with salt and pepper. Whisk with a fork to combine and pour it over the asparagus. Chop the egg and sprinkle it on top of the asparagus, followed by the parsley. Serve immediately.

celeriac *rémoulade*

1 lb. (1 large) celeriac, peeled

1 cup crème fraîche or sour cream

freshly squeezed juice ½ lemon

2 tablespoons whole grain mustard

a small handful flatleaf parsley, finely chopped (optional)

sea salt and freshly ground black pepper

SERVES 4–6

Coarsely shred the celeriac using a mandoline or food processor with a julienne attachment. Set aside.

To make the dressing, put the remaining ingredients in a medium bowl and season with salt and pepper. Whisk with a fork to combine. Add the celeriac and mix well until the celeriac is coated with the dressing. Check the seasoning and add more salt if necessary. Sprinkle with parsley (if using) and refrigerate until ready to serve.

blanched green beans
with hazelnuts and raspberry vinaigrette

10 oz. thin green beans, trimmed

3 tablespoons hazelnut or walnut oil

1 tablespoon raspberry vinegar

1 teaspoon Dijon mustard

1 shallot, finely chopped

¼ cup hazelnuts, toasted and chopped

sea salt and freshly ground black pepper

SERVES 4–6

Blanch the beans in a saucepan of salted boiling water. Drain and refresh in cold water. Pat dry with paper towels and arrange in a serving dish.

To make the dressing, put the oil, vinegar, mustard, and shallot in a small bowl and season with salt and pepper. Whisk with a fork to combine and pour it over the beans. Sprinkle the toasted hazelnuts on top and serve immediately.

cheese, half-dried tomato,
and black olive *gougères*

1 cup cold water

3 tablespoons butter, diced

1 cup plus 2 tablespoons all-purpose flour, sifted on to paper

4 small eggs

⅓ cup grated Gruyère cheese

10 black olives, pitted and chopped

4 half-dried tomatoes, finely chopped

1 garlic clove, finely chopped

sea salt

2–3 large baking sheets, greased

MAKES 30

Preheat the oven to 400°F. To make the choux pastry, place the cold water and butter in a large saucepan and add a pinch of salt. Bring to a boil, then remove from the heat and add the sifted flour, all at once. Beat the mixture with a wooden spoon or heat-resistant spatula and return the pan to the heat. Keep beating until the flour rolls off the sides of the saucepan and the mixture clings in a ball to the spoon. Remove the pan from the heat and quickly beat in the eggs, two at a time. The mixture should form a sticky ball. Add the cheese, olives, tomatoes, and garlic and mix gently. Using a teaspoon, put small balls of the dough on the greased baking sheets, spacing them well apart. Bake in the preheated oven for 20–25 minutes, until puffed up and golden brown. Serve immediately while still warm.

bacon-wrapped prunes
stuffed with almonds

12 large prunes, preferably Agen

24 whole unsalted almonds

8 thin slices of streaky bacon, each cut into 3 pieces

24 toothpicks

MAKES 24

Preheat the oven to 400°F. Break or cut the prunes in half and discard the pit. Take a prune half and firmly push an almond into it, wrapping the sides around so that it is cocooned. Wrap a piece of bacon around the prune and secure it with a toothpick. Repeat with the remaining prunes, almonds and bacon to make 24 pieces, placing them on a baking sheets as you go.

Bake in the preheated oven for about 5–6 minutes, until the bacon is crisp. Serve warm.

quick mini *pissaladières*

9 oz. frozen puff pastry dough, thawed

1½ lbs. yellow onions, thinly sliced

5 tablespoons olive oil

3 garlic cloves, finely chopped

1 tablespoon sugar

1 tablespoon white wine vinegar

1 tablespoon dried *Herbes de Provence*

2½ oz. anchovy fillets, halved lengthways

a small handful of black olives, pitted

sea salt and freshly ground black pepper

a pastry-cutter, 3 inches in diameter

MAKES 20

Preheat the oven to 400°F. Unroll the pastry dough and use a pastry-cutter to stamp out 20 circles. Refrigerate until needed. Heat the olive oil in a large saucepan. Add the onions and season well with salt and pepper. Cook over medium/high heat for about 10 minutes. Add the garlic, sugar, and vinegar. Reduce the heat to low and sauté gently for about 20 minutes, until the onions have caramelized. Remove the pan from the heat. Place the pastry circles on baking sheets and divide the onion mixture between them. Arrange the anchovies on top, sprinkle with the herbs, and add a few olives. Bake in the preheated oven for 25 minutes, until crisp. Serve warm.

French seafood platter
"fruits de mer"

Seafood lovers will be thrilled with this luxurious shellfish *plateau de fruits de mer*, literally "fruits of the sea." This is a favorite in Parisian brasseries, where tables of guests will work their way through an enormous seafood platter, washed down with several bottles of chilled Muscadet or Champagne. Plenty of crushed ice is key to impressive presentation and do supply shellfish crackers, seafood forks, finger bowls, and piles of napkins for your guests. If you find seafood a little intimidating, ask your fishmonger to do most of the work for you. This menu is simplicity itself, as all you need do is set the table and make a few quick and delicious sauces.

TO BUY

- Lobster tails and/or claws
- Crab claws and/or legs
- Langoustines and/or unshelled king or jumbo shrimp
- Raw oysters or clams and steamed mussels
- Plenty of good-quality baguette or a French sourdough bread, such as *pain au levain*
- Good-quality mayonnaise
- Little pots of unsalted French butter
- A bottle of Tabasco sauce
- Lemon wedges for squeezing
- Sprigs of fresh parsley to garnish

TO MAKE (see recipes page 51)

- Spicy citrus and cilantro salsa
- Shallot vinegar
- Classic American cocktail sauce
- Lime and caper mayonnaise

Or you could also try:

- Saffron and garlic aïoli (see page 21)

spicy citrus and cilantro salsa

freshly squeezed juice and zest of 1 unwaxed lime and 1 lemon

5 tablespoons olive oil

2 tablespoons finely chopped fresh cilantro

2 medium green chiles, finely chopped

1 tablespoon sugar

sea salt and freshly ground black pepper

MAKES 1 CUP

Put all the ingredients in a bowl and season with salt and pepper. Refrigerate until ready to serve. This keeps for two days, refrigerated.

shallot vinegar

2 shallots, peeled and finely diced

½ cup red wine vinegar

sea salt and freshly ground black pepper

MAKES ⅔ CUP

Put the shallots and vinegar in a bowl and whisk with a fork to combine. Season with salt and pepper. This keeps for two days, refrigerated.

lime and caper mayonnaise

2 egg yolks, at room temperature

1 teaspoon Dijon mustard

¾ cup grapeseed or sunflower oil

1 tablespoon small capers, roughly chopped

freshly squeezed juice and zest of 1 unwaxed lime

½ teaspoon each salt and pepper

MAKES 1¼ CUPS

Put the egg yolks, mustard, salt, and pepper in a bowl and whisk with a fork or balloon whisk to combine. Slowly drizzle in the oil, whisking continuously, until it is incorporated. Add the capers, lime juice, and zest and whisk again. This keeps for up to four days, refrigerated.

classic American cocktail sauce

½ cup tomato ketchup

¼ cup freshly grated or prepared horseradish

freshly squeezed juice of 1 lemon

1 tablespoon Worcestershire sauce

1 tablespoon finely chopped celery rib

sea salt and freshly ground black pepper

MAKES ¾ CUP

Put all the ingredients in a bowl and whisk with a fork to combine. Season with salt and pepper. This keeps for up to four days, refrigerated.

Greek meze

Spain has tapas; Greece and the eastern Mediterranean have *mezethes*. These delicious little plates of spicy, savory, and often salty food are designed to enhance the taste of alcoholic drinks and provide a backdrop to a social gathering. In Greece, groups of family and friends will gather together or go out for *mezethes*, a drink, conversation, and laughter. If you are fortunate enough to have a Greek or Cypriot shop close to you, that is where you will find the creamiest feta, seeded breads, and typical ingredients, such as dried wild oregano. Present your meze in fresh white and blue dishes and serve with tumblers of aniseed-flavored ouzo or a delicious Greek wine. Some of the best come from the island of Santorini.

TO BUY

- *Hummus* (chickpea dip)
- *Tzatziki* (cucumber yoghurt dip))
- *Taramasalata* (salted cod's roe dip)
- *Dolmades* (stuffed vine leaves), zucchini fritters, and cheese pies
- Marinated octopus salad
- Greek-style green and black olives marinated with oregano
- Mini pita breads and *daktyla*, a soft, white, Greek-style loaf topped with sesame, black onion, or anise seeds

TO PREPARE

- A simple Greek-style salad of tomato, cucumber, and feta with black olives, dressed with equal amounts of freshly squeezed lemon juice and olive oil and sprinkled with dried oregano
- Lightly steamed greens, such as Swiss chard or spinach, with a squeeze of lemon juice, a drizzle of olive oil, and a pinch of cinnamon
- Wedges of watermelon, or cubes of watermelon threaded on to toothpicks with cubes of feta

TO COOK (see recipes pages 54–55)

- Spicy baked feta
- Roasted eggplant and caper dip
- Swordfish souvlaki bites
- Shrimp salad with dill
- Pan-fried halloumi (*saganaki*)

You could also try:

- Spinach, cinnamon and pine nut phyllo cigars (see page 36)
- Warm halloumi bites (see page 36)

spicy baked feta

6½ oz. feta

3 tablespoons olive oil

a pinch of dried oregano

½ teaspoon dried red pepper flakes

sea salt and freshly ground black pepper

lemon wedges, to serve

aluminium foil

SERVES 4–6

Preheat the oven to 400°F. Lay out the foil on a baking sheet. Put the feta on the foil, sprinkle with the oregano and red pepper flakes and drizzle with the olive oil. Season with a little salt and pepper. Close the foil to make a sealed package. Place the tray in the preheated oven and bake the feta for about 20 minutes. Be careful when opening the foil, as hot steam will escape.

Serve immediately with lemon wedges on the side for squeezing.

roasted eggplant and caper dip

1 small red onion, finely chopped

freshly squeezed juice of 1 lemon

2 large eggplants

2 ripe plum tomatoes, peeled and diced

1 garlic clove, finely chopped

1 teaspoon small capers

1 scallion, chopped

¼ cup olive oil

2 tablespoons finely chopped flatleaf parsley

sea salt and freshly ground black pepper

toasted pita bread, to serve

SERVES 4–6

Preheat the oven to 350°F. Put the onion in a small bowl and pour in the lemon juice. Set aside. Prick the eggplants all over with a fork and put them directly on the oven shelf. Roast them in the preheated oven for just under 1 hour, turning them over occasionally. When cool enough to handle, carefully peel off the blackened skin and discard it along with the stalks. Chop the flesh and put it in a large bowl. Add the onion, tomatoes, garlic, capers, scallion, olive oil, and parsley. Season with salt and pepper and mix well. Serve with toasted pita bread for dipping.

swordfish souvlaki bites

2 swordfish or tuna steaks

lemon wedges, to serve

sea salt and freshly ground black pepper

FOR THE MARINADE:

1 anchovy fillet, rinsed of oil

10 small capers

2 tablespoons fresh oregano, finely chopped or 1 teaspoon dried

1 garlic clove, finely chopped

3 tablespoons red wine vinegar

5 tablespoons extra-virgin olive oil

12 wooden skewers, soaked in water for 15 minutes

MAKES 12

Put all the ingredients for the marinade in a large bowl. Cut the fish into bite-size cubes and add them to the bowl. Cover and refrigerate for 30 minutes, but no longer. Thread two cubes of fish on each skewer and season with salt and pepper. Heat a stovetop grill pan or outdoor grill. Grill the fish for 1–2 minutes on each side, until cooked through. Serve warm, with a little of the marinade spooned over the top and lemon wedges on the side for squeezing.

shrimp salad with dill

10 oz. large cooked shrimp, peeled

2 ribs celery, finely diced

1 small red onion, finely diced

2 tablespoons finely chopped fresh dill

2 *peperoncini* (pickled chile peppers), finely diced

freshly squeezed juice and zest of 1 unwaxed lemon

4 tablespoons extra-virgin olive oil

sea salt and freshly ground black pepper

SERVES 4–6

Put the shrimp, celery, onion, dill, and peperoncini in a bowl. To make the dressing, put the olive oil and lemon juice in a bowl and season with salt and pepper. Whisk with a fork to combine. Pour the dressing over the salad and toss well before serving.

pan-fried halloumi
saganaki

4 tablespoons all-purpose flour

8 oz. halloumi cheese

3 tablespoons olive oil

2 tablespoons ouzo

sea salt and freshly ground black pepper

lemon wedges, to serve

SERVES 4–6

Put the flour on a plate and season with salt and pepper. Cut the halloumi into eight slices. Dip each one into the flour to coat. Set aside.

Preheat the oven to 225°F and put a plate in to warm. Heat 1½ tablespoons of the olive oil in a large skillet. When very hot, carefully add the cheese slices to the pan, four at a time. Fry the cheese for about 1 minute on each side, until golden brown. Add 1 tablespoon ouzo to the pan and light with a match. It will burn out quickly and when it does, remove the pan from the heat and transfer the cheese to the warmed plate and back into the cool oven until ready to serve.

Pour the remaining olive oil in to the pan and repeat with the other four slices. Serve warm, with lemon wedges on the side for squeezing.

Italian "verdura" antipasti

These colorful and delicious *antipasti* are the perfect solution to entertaining vegetarian friends and popular with meat-eaters too. The Italians have a special way with vegetables—no wonder, when their produce is so ripe and flavorful. Italian delis and gourmet shops carry a dazzling array of grilled, roasted, and marinated vegetables which are just waiting to be put together in this way. Buy a good selection of tasty Italian breads—such as ciabatta and focaccia—looking out for the ones enriched with olives, herbs, and sun-dried tomatoes. Serve with the classic Italian aperitif, Campari, with soda or orange juice and plenty of ice.

TO BUY

- *Bocconcini* (mini mozzarella balls) or balls of fresh buffalo mozzarella

- Baby antipasto-style mushrooms and half-dried tomatoes marinated in oil

- Slices of grilled or roasted eggplant, zucchini, and red bell peppers

- *Cippoline agrodulce* (little onions pickled in sweet balsamic vinegar)

- Italian-style green and black olives

- Large caperberries on stalks

- Fresh basil leaves, to garnish

- A good selection of rustic Italian breads including *focaccia* and *ciabatta*

TO PREPARE

- Cooked borlotti or cannellini beans mixed with baby arugula and tossed in freshly squeezed lemon juice and olive oil

- A simple salad of shaved raw fennel and radicchio drizzled with olive oil and balsamic vinegar

- A plate of sliced plum tomatoes and red onions sprinkled with chopped fresh basil and drizzled with olive oil

TO COOK (see recipes page 59)

- Roasted butternut squash with mint and pine nuts

- Celery and mushroom salad with Parmesan and lemon dressing

- Gorgonzola and pear bruschetta

roasted butternut squash
with mint and pinenuts

2¼ lbs. butternut squash, cubed

5 tablespoons extra-virgin olive oil

2 garlic cloves, thinly sliced

1 small red onion, thinly sliced

1½ tablespoons honey

3 tablespoons red wine vinegar

½ teaspoon dried red pepper flakes

2 tablespoons chopped fresh mint

¼ cup pine nuts, toasted

sea salt and freshly ground black pepper

SERVES 4–6

Preheat the oven to 400ºF. Place the squash pieces on a baking sheet. Drizzle with 2–3 tablespoons of the olive oil and toss to coat. Season with salt and pepper. Bake the squash in the preheated oven for about 20 minutes, until golden and tender.

Heat the remaining oil in a large skillet. Add the garlic and gently sauté until light brown. Add the onion, honey, vinegar, and red pepper flakes. Bring to a boil, reduce the heat and simmer for about 2 minutes, until the sauce is syrupy. Transfer the cooked squash to a large serving dish. Spoon the warm dressing over the top and sprinkle with chopped mint and toasted pine nuts. Serve warm.

celery and mushroom
salad with Parmesan and lemon dressing

1 head celery with outer ribs removed (leaving heart only), thinly sliced

7 oz. small cremini mushrooms, washed and thinly sliced

1 small red onion, diced

freshly squeezed juice of 1 lemon

5 tablespoons extra-virgin olive oil

¼ cup finely grated Parmesan

sea salt and freshly ground black pepper

SERVES 4–6

Put the celery, mushrooms, and onion in a large bowl. Put the lemon juice and olive oil in a small bowl and whisk with a fork to combine. Season well with salt and pepper.

Add the Parmesan and stir. Pour the dressing over the salad and toss well. Serve with bread for mopping up the dressing.

Gorgonzola and
pear bruschetta

1 ripe pear, washed

1 tablespoon freshly squeezed lemon juice

6 slices ciabatta bread

2 oz. Gorgonzola cheese

a handful of baby arugula

balsamic vinegar, to drizzle

freshly ground black pepper

MAKES 6

Leave the skin on the pear and slice it lengthwise. Place the slices in a bowl and add the lemon juice. Set aside. Toast the bread on both sides until lightly golden.

Spread each piece with a tablespoon of Gorgonzola and top with a slice of pear. Add a few arugula leaves and drizzle with balsamic vinegar. Season with pepper and serve warm.

Mediterranean cheeseboard

Cheeseboards are simple to assemble and always popular. A specialist cheese shop is the ideal place to go, but most supermarkets now carry a good range. Choose a selection of flavors ranging from creamy through to piquant, and a variety of textures too: velvet-soft goat cheese, gooey Camembert, and a firm Comté, for example. Different cheeses are complemented by both fresh and dried fruits, so offer these alongside. Buy good-quality crackers and serve them in a cloth-lined basket. Display your choices attractively on a wooden board or wicker tray. Serve with a dry Sauvignon Blanc or a fruity red, such as Merlot.

TO BUY IN

- Gorgonzola or other soft blue cheese
- Firm goat cheese such as *crottin de Chavignol*
- A wedge of Brie
- Camembert (packed in an attractive round wooden box)
- French Comté or a similar dense Swiss cheese such as Gruyère
- Pecorino or Parmesan
- Fresh red and green grapes
- Fresh cherries
- Ripe pears
- Fresh or dried apple slices
- Fresh figs
- Medjool dates
- *Membrillo* (Spanish quince preserve)
- Large Muscat raisins
- Walnuts (shell on)
- Spiced fruit chutneys
- A good selection of crackers, including water biscuits and whole-grain varieties
- Some enriched breads (such as walnut and raisin bread) and some good-quality baguettes or French sourdough bread such as *pain au levain*

TO MAKE (see recipes on page 62)

- Spiced fig jam
- Fresh tomato chutney

spiced fig jam

4 oz. dried ready-to-eat figs

2 tablespoons olive oil

1 small red onion, diced

freshly squeezed juice and zest of 1 unwaxed lemon

¼ cup sherry vinegar

1 teaspoon ground cinnamon

½ teaspoon freshly grated nutmeg

½ teaspoon cumin seeds

½ teaspoon cayenne pepper

5 tablespoons superfine sugar

sea salt and freshly ground black pepper

MAKES 1¼ CUPS

Pour 1 cup boiling water over the figs and let them sit for 10 minutes. Drain in a colander (reserving the soaking liquid) and when cool enough to handle chop them and set aside. Put the olive oil in a large skillet and add the onion. Sauté for about 5 minutes, until soft. Add the spices and season with salt and pepper. Add the figs, soaking liquid, vinegar, sugar, lemon juice and zest and simmer for for about 30 minutes, until the mixture is the consistency of jam. When cool, spoon into a sterilized resealable container. The jam will keep for up to one month, refrigerated.

fresh tomato chutney

2 x 14-oz. cans whole Italian plum tomatoes

1 large white or yellow onion, chopped

½ cup cider vinegar

½ cup superfine sugar

3 tablespoons golden raisins

2 teaspoons mustard seeds

½ teaspoon ground allspice

½ teaspoon ground cinnamon

4 cardamom pods, crushed

½ teaspoon cayenne pepper

sea salt and freshly ground black pepper

MAKES 1¼ CUPS

Put all the ingredients in a large saucepan and season with salt and pepper. Bring to a boil, reduce the heat and gently cook over medium/low heat for about 40 minutes, using a a flat spoon to break up the tomatoes. It is ready when the mixture has reduced and is the consistency of jam. When cool, spoon into a sterilized resealable container. The chutney will keep for up to one month, refrigerated.

index

conversion chart

Weights and measures have been rounded up
or down slightly to make measuring easier.

Volume equivalents:

American	Metric	Imperial
1 teaspoon	5 ml	
1 tablespoon	15 ml	
¼ cup	60 ml	2 fl.oz.
⅓ cup	75 ml	2½ fl.oz.
½ cup	125 ml	4 fl.oz.
⅔ cup	150 ml	5 fl.oz. (¼ pint)
¾ cup	175 ml	6 fl.oz.
1 cup	250 ml	8 fl.oz.

Weight equivalents: **Measurements:**

Imperial	Metric	Inches	Cm
1 oz.	30 g	¼ inch	5 mm
2 oz.	55 g	½ inch	1 cm
3 oz.	85 g	¾ inch	1.5 cm
3½ oz.	100 g	1 inch	2.5 cm
4 oz.	115 g	2 inches	5 cm
5 oz.	140 g	3 inches	7 cm
6 oz.	175 g	4 inches	10 cm
8 oz. (½ lb.)	225 g	5 inches	12 cm
9 oz.	250 g	6 inches	15 cm
10 oz.	280 g	7 inches	18 cm
11½ oz.	325 g	8 inches	20 cm
12 oz.	350 g	9 inches	23 cm
13 oz.	375 g	10 inches	25 cm
14 oz.	400 g	11 inches	28 cm
15 oz.	425 g	12 inches	30 cm
16 oz. (1 lb.)	450 g		